A Guide for Using

The Breadwinner

in the Classroom

Based on the novel written by Deborah Ellis

This guide written by
Melissa Hart, M.F.A.

Teacher Created Resources, Inc.
6421 Industry Way
Westminster, CA 92683
www.teachercreated.com

ISBN: 978-1-4206-2216-4

© 2008 Teacher Created Resources, Inc.
Made in U.S.A.

Edited by
Heather Douglas
Illustrated by
Clint McKnight
Cover Art by
Courtney Barnes

Table of Contents

Introduction

A good book can enrich our lives like a good friend. Fictional characters can inspire us and teach us about the world in which we live. We can turn to books for companionship, entertainment, and guidance. A truly beloved book may touch our lives forever.

Great care has been taken with Literature Units to select books that are sure to become your students' good friends!

Teachers who use this unit will find the following features to supplement their own ideas:

- Sample Lesson Plans

- Pre-reading activities

- A biographical sketch and picture of the author

- Vocabulary lists and suggested vocabulary activities

- Chapters are grouped for study. Each section includes the following:

  — quiz

  — hands-on project

  — cooperative learning activity

  — cross-curricular connection

  — extension into the reader's life

- Post-reading activities

- Book report ideas

- Research activities

- Culminating activities

- Three different options for unit tests

- Bibliography of related reading

- Answer key

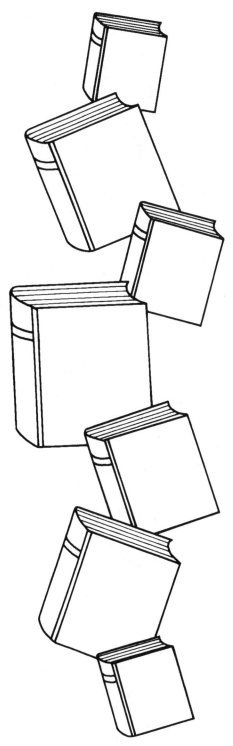

We are certain this unit will be a valuable addition to your own curriculum ideas to supplement *The Breadwinner.*

Standards

Each page in *A Guide for Using* The Breadwinner *in the Classroom* meets one or more of the following fifth-grade standards, which are used with permission from McREL (Copyright 2007, McREL, Mid-continent Research for Education and Learning. Telephone: 303/337-0990. Website: *www.mcrel.org*).

Language Arts Standards	Page Number
Uses the general skills and strategies of the writing process.	9, 10, 12, 13, 14, 15, 17, 18, 19, 20, 24, 25, 27, 28, 29, 30, 34, 35, 36, 37, 41, 42, 43
Uses the stylistic and rhetorical aspects of writing.	9, 14, 18, 19, 24, 27, 29, 34, 36, 37, 38
Uses grammatical and mechanical conventions in written compositions.	24, 37, 38
Gathers and uses information for research purposes	11, 12, 17, 22, 23, 26, 27, 28, 32, 33, 35, 36
Uses the general skills and strategies of the reading process.	5, 6, 7, 8, 9, 10, 15, 20, 25, 30
Uses listening and speaking strategies for different purposes.	9, 13, 22, 32, 35, 39, 40
Understands the characteristics and components of the media.	13, 17, 27, 28

Sample Lesson Plan

The time it takes to complete the suggested lessons below will vary, depending on the type of activity, and your students' abilities and interest levels.

Lesson 1

- Introduce and complete some or all of the pre-reading activities from "Before Reading the Book." (page 6)
- Read "About the Author" with students. (page 7)
- Introduce the vocabulary list for Section 1. (page 9)

Lesson 2

- Read Chapters 1–3. As you read, place the vocabulary words in the context of the book and discuss their meanings.
- Locate Afghanistan on the classroom map. Then locate Kabul and Mazar-E-Sharif. Parvana and her family live in Kabul and travel to Mazar-E-Sharif.
- Chose a vocabulary activity to complete. (page 10)
- Complete "Nan Bread" (page 12).
- Research Afghan history (page 13).
- Learn about Afghan cultures (page 14).
- Explore emotions (page 15).
- Administer the Section 1 Quiz. (page 11)
- Introduce the vocabulary list for Section 2. (page 9)

Lesson 3

- Read Chapters 4–6. As you read, place the vocabulary words in the context of the book and discuss their meanings.
- Choose a vocabulary activity to complete. (page 10)
- Make a puzzle (page 17).
- Explore gender in literature and film (page 18).
- Learn the power of language (page 19).
- Examine your family role (page 20).
- Administer the Section 2 Quiz. (page 16)
- Introduce the vocabulary list for Section 3. (page 9)

Lesson 4

- Read Chapters 7–9. As you read, place the vocabulary words in the context of the book and discuss their meanings.
- Choose a vocabulary activity to complete. (page 10)

- Learn to embroider (page 22).
- Create a marketplace (page 24).
- Examine your water (page 25).
- Write a letter (page 26).
- Administer the Section 3 Quiz. (page 21)
- Introduce the vocabulary list for Section 4. (page 9)

Lesson 5

- Read Chapters 10–12. As you read, place the vocabulary words in the context of the book and discuss their meanings.
- Choose a vocabulary activity to complete. (page 10)
- Plant a flower garden (page 28).
- Make a magazine (page 29).
- Research land mines (page 30).
- Explore your own actions (page 31).
- Administer the Section 4 Quiz. (page 27)
- Introduce the vocabulary list for Section 5. (page 9)

Lesson 6

- Read Chapters 13–15. As you read, place the vocabulary words in the context of the book and discuss their meanings.
- Choose a vocabulary activity to complete. (page 10)
- Learn to dry apricots (page 33).
- Lend a helping hand (page 34).
- Draw Afghan clothing (page 35).
- Compare yourself to a character (page 36).
- Administer the Section 5 Quiz. (page 32)

Lesson 7

- Discuss questions students have about the book. (page 37)
- Assign a book report and research activity. (pages 38–39)
- Begin work on one or more culminating activities. (pages 40–42)

Lesson 8

- Choose and administer Unit Tests: 1, 2, and/or 3. (pages 43–45)
- Discuss students' feelings about the book.
- Provide a bibliography of related reading (page 46).

Before Reading the Book

Before you begin reading *The Breadwinner* with your students, complete one or more of the following pre-reading activities to stimulate their interest and enhance their comprehension.

1. Examine the cover of the book. Ask students to predict the book's plot, characters, and setting.

2. Discuss the title. Ask students what they think *The Breadwinner* means, and see if they can predict anything about the book from its title.

3. Answer these questions:

   • What would it be like to lose a sister or brother?

   • What might it be like to be forbidden to go outside except covered by heavy clothing such as a burqa and/or chador?

   • What challenges would you experience if you had to live in just one room with your family?

   • How would you feel if soldiers took away one of your parents?

   • What do you know about Afghanistan? the Taliban?

   • What sacrifices would you be willing to make to take care of your family?

   • What would it be like to pretend to be a person of the other gender?

   • What are your feelings about war?

4. Direct students to work in groups or brainstorm what it means to be a hero/heroine. Share your suggestions with the class.

5. Direct students to work in groups to list the various rights that they have as U.S. citizens in terms of clothing, school, the freedom to travel, and even the freedom to shop.

6. Brainstorm the different ways in which students might help their parents to take care of the family. Think in terms of taking on chores and responsibilities, and also in terms of particular behaviors which might help parents.

7. Work in groups to discuss war in the Middle East. Ask students to list everything they know about Afghanistan and the infringements on human rights in that country. Ask them to list prejudices that they, and/or others, might have against Afghan people, and encourage them to discuss how best to overcome these prejudices.

About the Author

Deborah Ellis was born in Ontario, Canada, on August 7th, 1960. She has one sister who is two years older. When Deborah was still quite young, her family moved to the small town of Paris in Ontario. As a child growing up, Deborah spent a great deal of time alone. She loved to read. She enjoyed books that took place in New York City, such as *Harriet the Spy* and *A Tree Grows in Brooklyn*. She also enjoyed reading books by E.B. White and Lewis Carroll.

At age 11 or 12, Deborah realized she wanted to be an author. She wrote poems and plays and sent them to magazines and writing contests. She was so skilled at writing and reading that she took high-school English when she was still in eighth grade.

Deborah also loved to ride her bicycle around town. She'd pack a lunch and disappear into the hills. She enjoyed building forts and wandering around her town's graveyard. She admits that as a child she was isolated from her peers. "Loners are loners, and that's kind of a universal thing," she once told a magazine writer. "People feel like they're on the outside, and they don't have a sense that they can change their circumstances."

However, in high school, Deborah realized she *could* change the world. She joined the Peace Movement, graduated, and moved to Toronto to work in politics. She joined the feminist movements, and campaigned for women's rights.

When she was 25, Deborah wrote a play that won $1,500 in a competition. She decided to write a book for children because of another writing contest. The book, *Looking for X*, won the 2000 Governor General's Literary Award.

When she's not writing, Deborah works as a mental-health counselor. She has traveled to Afghanistan to interview women in refugee camps. In one of the camps, she met a mother who inspired her to write *The Breadwinner*. This book is the first in a trilogy; the other two novels are *Parvana's Journey,* and *Mud City*. She donates part of the proceeds from her books to UNICEF and Street Kids International. Her latest book is *I Am a Taxi*, which is about a boy from Bolivia.

Deborah says that in writing a book, she often starts with a question. As you read *The Breadwinner,* ask yourself what question might have inspired Deborah to write this book.

The Breadwinner

by Deborah Ellis

(Groundwood, 2000)

Eleven-year-old Parvana is allowed out of the house because she is small for her age. While her mother and older sister must hide in their family's one room according to the laws of the Taliban, Parvana accompanies her disabled father to the marketplace. Although her father taught history, and her mother worked as a writer, Parvana's parents are now poor because of the Taliban's restrictions.

One night, soldiers take custody of Parvana's father and beat her mother. Parvana and her mother try to get Father released from prison. They return home injured and disappointed. Mother falls into a depression, and Parvana and her siblings run out of food. Finally, Parvana's sister makes her go out for bread. A soldier beats Parvana, who flees. She meets her mother's friend, Mrs. Weera.

chador   burqa

Mrs. Weera discovers how Parvana and her family are living and decides that Parvana must dress like a boy to obtain food and water, and protect the family. Parvana reluctantly agrees.

Dressed as a boy, Parvana discovers freedom outside her family's room. She reads letters and sells objects for money. In the marketplace, Parvana begins to find strange objects left for her. She meets a school friend, also dressed as a boy, working to pay for food.

Mrs. Weera and Parvana's mother start a newspaper. They also start a school for girls. Parvana and her friend ponder a way to make more money for their families.

They take on a horrifying job to buy trays from which they can sell candy and cigarettes. While at a stadium, they see a terrifying sight. Parvana skips work until the family runs out of food. She returns to work, then goes home to find that her sister is getting married.

Parvana's mother says the family must travel to north Afghanistan, where Parvana's sister will live after marriage. Parvana refuses to go. Her mother leaves her in Kabul with Mrs. Weera. Parvana says good–bye to her family as they leave on their months-long trip—a trip which turns out to be dangerous.

While taking refuge in a building, Parvana meets a woman who has just come from northern Afghanistan. The woman gives her unsettling news, but Parvana is cheered by the return of her father. She realizes that she has gained new confidence, and she feels a new hope for both her future and the future of her country.

Vocabulary Lists

Below are lists of vocabulary words for each section of chapters in *The Breadwinner*. Note that the novel contains a glossary at the back.

The following page offers ideas for using this vocabulary in classroom activities.

Section 1 (Chapters 1–3)

chador	burqa	nan
Taliban	toshak	hospitable
forbid(ade)	looter(s)	veil
hawk(ed)	shalwar kameez	turban
decree(d)	land mine	illiterate

Section 2 (Chapters 4–6)

preoccupied	sensible	warily
basin	pakul	sulk
glare	bold(ly)	brusque(ly)
washroom	union	gingerly
consider(ed)	eternity	gruff

Section 3 (Chapters 7–9)

Pashtu	labyrinth	latrine
embed(ded)	dawdling	escort
bargain	sympathy	distinguish
counter-offer	Karachi	kerosene
vibrant	raid(s)	smuggle

Section 4 (Chapters 10–12)

stench	ancestors	booty
stingy	relent(ed)	nomad(s)
unearthed	gleeful(ly)	snippet(s)
mascot	sting	fertile
accommodate	intimidate(d)	

Section 5 (Chapters 13–15)

territory	evidence	bride-price
curfew	prod(ding)	refugee
down(ed)	drawn	exile
heroine	cropped	nutrients
corridor(s)	poultice	derision

Vocabulary Activities

You can help your students learn the vocabulary words in *The Breadwinner* by providing them with the stimulating vocabulary activities below.

1. Ask students to work in groups to create an **Illustrated Book** of the vocabulary words and their meanings.

2. Group students. Direct groups to use vocabulary words to create **Crossword Puzzles** and **Word Searches**. Groups can trade puzzles with each other, complete them, then check each other's work.

3. Play **Guess the Definition**. One student writes down the correct definition of the vocabulary word. The others write down false definitions, close enough to the original definition that their classmates might be fooled. Read all definitions, and then challenge students to guess the correct one. The students whose definitions mislead their classmates get a point for each student fooled.

4. Use the word in five different sentences. Compare sentences and discuss.

5. Write a **Short Story** using as many of the words as possible. Students may then read their stories in groups.

6. Encourage your students to use each new vocabulary word in a conversation five times during one day. They can take notes on how and when the word was used, and then share their experiences with the class.

7. Play **Vocabulary Charades**. Each student or group of students gets a word to act out. Other students must guess the word.

8. Play **Vocabulary Pictures**. Each student or group of students must draw a picture representing a word on the chalkboard or on paper. Other students must guess the word.

9. Challenge students to a **Vocabulary Bee**. In groups or separately, students must spell the word correctly and give its proper definition.

10. Talk about **Parts of Speech** by discussing the different forms that a word may take. For instance, some words may function as nouns, as well as verbs. The word "escort" is a good example of a word that can be both a noun and a verb. Some words that look alike may have different meanings; for example, in *The Breadwinner*, the word "drawn" is used to describe someone who looks pale and ill, but it may also be used to describe an object that has been sketched on paper.

11. Ask your students to make **Flash Cards** with the word printed on one side and the definition printed on the other. Ask students to work with a younger class to help them learn the definitions of the new words, using the flash cards.

12. Create **Word Art** by writing the words with glue on stiff paper, and then cover the glue with glitter or sand. Alternatively, students may write the words with a squeeze bottle full of jam on bread to create an edible lesson.

Quiz Time

Answer the following questions about chapters 1–3.

1. Why isn't Parvana supposed to be outside?

_____

_____

2. In what ways does Parvana's father try to make money?

_____

_____

3. Why does Parvana's family live together in one small room?

_____

_____

4. Why is Parvana the only person in her family who can fetch water?

_____

_____

5. How are Afghans supposed to treat a guest, according to Father?

_____

_____

6. Who is Malali, and why is she important in Afghan history?

_____

_____

7. Why do the Taliban take Father away?

_____

_____

8. Why is Parvana afraid that if she loses track of her mother on the street, she'll never find her again?

_____

_____

Nan Bread

"The family ate Afghan-style, sitting around a plastic cloth spread out on the floor. Food cheered everyone up, and the family lingered after the meal was over."

Parvana and her family eat nan—a type of yeasted flat bread served with hot meals. Nan is cooked in a *tandoor*, or clay oven. It resembles pita bread, but is slightly softer.

Note: Please check for food allergies before using this recipe.

Nan Bread

Ingredients

- 2 cups warm water
- 2 tsp salt
- 4 T unsalted butter
- 2 T honey
- 2 T dry yeast
- 5 ½ cups whole-wheat flour

Materials

- large mixing bowl
- kitchen towel
- mixing spoon
- rolling pin
- board for kneading
- baking sheets

Directions

1. Put warm water in mixing bowl. Stir butter into warm water until it melts.

2. Add yeast and salt and stir until dissolved. Cover bowl with damp kitchen towel. Set aside for 10 minutes.

3. Stir in honey, then add just enough flour to make a soft, pliable dough.

4. Flour your board and place dough on it. Knead the dough until it feels elastic and smooth.

5. Put dough back in mixing bowl. Cover with kitchen towel and let dough rise for half an hour.

6. Preheat oven to 400°F.

7. Put dough on floured board and knead for one minute. Then, form it into 24 balls.

8. Roll each ball out to ¼" thickness. Let them rise on floured board for 15 minutes.

9. Grease baking sheets. Place pieces 1" apart on sheets and bake for 10 minutes or until lightly browned.

Serves 24

History of Afghanistan

Parvana's father was a history professor before he lost his job, and history is Parvana's favorite subject. The first three chapters of *The Breadwinner* cover a great deal about the complicated history of Afghanistan. In order to further understand this country's history, work together with 2–4 of your classmates to create a time line of important events.

Materials

- a six-foot piece of butcher paper, one per group
- markers or crayons
- encyclopedias, books, or computers for research
- several pieces of scratch paper
- a pen or pencil

Directions

1. First, research the history of Afghanistan. You know from *The Breadwinner* that the Soviet Union invaded the country before the Taliban took it over. Farther back in history, Afghanistan had been home to Persians, Greeks, Arabs, Turks, and the British. Make notes on what your group considers the most important events in Afghan history.

2. Now, create your time line. On the piece of butcher paper, chart important historical events from the formation of Afghanistan until today. You may choose to make your time line vertical or horizontal. Feel free to illustrate your time line with pictures as well.

3. Display your time line on the wall. Compare it with those time lines made by other groups in your class. Discuss the following questions:

   - Why have so many countries been interested in conquering Afghanistan?
   - How would you describe Afghan history?
   - How do you think Parvana's family feels about the history of their country?

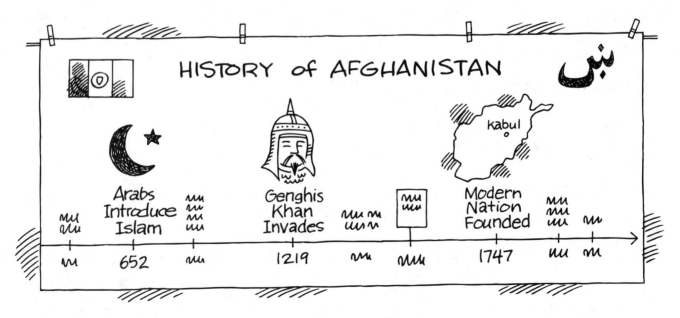

Afghan Culture

The previous page asks you to create a time line of Afghanistan's history. But this country is more than just a record of its invasions and wars.

By yourself or in groups of 2–3, answer the questions below about Afghanistan. Use encyclopedias, books, and the Internet to do your research.

1. On what continent is Afghanistan located? What countries are its closest neighbors?

_____

_____

2. What languages are spoken in Afghanistan?

_____

_____

3. What types of sports are played in this country?

_____

_____

4. Why is poetry important in Afghanistan?

_____

_____

5. What is education like for people your age in this country?

_____

_____

6. What types of foods do people eat in Afghanistan?

_____

_____

7. What kinds of animals would you find in this country?

_____

_____

8. Briefly describe the geography of Afghanistan.

_____

_____

Emotions: Same and Different

Parvana must deal with many emotions in her life. Some of these may be similar to feelings you have experienced. Fill out the following chart with specific details to show why Parvana experiences each emotion in chapters 1–3. Then, explain in what way you have felt each emotion at some point in your life. How are you similar to Parvana? How are you different?

Emotion	Parvana	You
loneliness	She is not allowed to play with other kids, and no one in her family is her age.	
resentment		
anger		
fear		
happiness		

Quiz Time

Answer the following questions about chapters 4–6.

1. Why does Father want Mother to go out into the city?

   _____

   _____

2. Why does Mother sleep for so long and stay silent?

   _____

   _____

3. Why does Parvana finally go out in search of food?

   _____

   _____

4. Why does the Taliban solider hit Parvana with a stick?

   _____

   _____

5. How did Mother and Mrs. Weera meet?

   _____

   _____

6. Why does the family, along with Mrs. Weera, decide to turn Parvana into a boy?

   _____

   _____

7. What discoveries does Parvana make the first time she goes out dressed as a boy?

   _____

   _____

8. Why does Parvana have to look like a boy inside the house, when she is with her family?

   _____

   _____

Puzzle Face

"Parvana remembered the pieces of photograph and got them out. Her father's face was like a jigsaw puzzle. She spread the pieces out on the mat in front of her. Maryam joined her and helped her put them in order."

You can create a jigsaw puzzle from the photograph of someone who is important to you.

Materials

- one photograph, preferably on photo paper
- posterboard slightly larger than your photograph
- scissors or craft knife
- rubber cement
- black marker
- envelope large enough for your puzzle pieces
- laminating machine (optional)

Directions

1. Place your photograph on the piece of posterboard. Carefully cut the board to fit the photo.

2. Coat the posterboard with rubber cement. Coat the back of your photograph with rubber cement, as well. When both are dry, gently press your photo onto the posterboard.

3. With black marker, draw outlines of puzzle pieces directly on the photograph.

4. You may opt to turn your puzzle over and write a note, or the name of the person in the photograph. (For example, you might write, "My father, in a photo taken June 25, 2007.")

5. Optional: At this point, you can ask your teacher to laminate your puzzle for greater durability. Do not attempt to laminate by yourself. The machine is hot!

6. Cut (or rip, as in the story) out puzzle pieces.

   Now you have a puzzle showing someone important to you. You can store the pieces in an envelope and pull them out whenever you want to remember this person.

The Big Switch

In Chapter six of *The Breadwinner,* Parvana's family decides to turn her into a boy so that she can shop for and protect her family. This idea of a main character in a book posing as the opposite gender isn't new. It's a technique that has been around for at least 500 years!

Directions: In groups of three or four, research the following plays, novels, and movies. Briefly describe the main character and why he or she switches gender in each story. The first one has been done for you.

1. ***Some Like It Hot*** (movie): *Joe and Jerry witness a Mafia massacre. Scared for their lives, they pretend to be female musicians in a woman's band so that the Mafia won't find them.*

   _____

   _____

   _____

2. ***The Ballad of Mulan*** (Chinese poem):

   _____

   _____

   _____

3. ***Tootsie*** (movie):

   _____

   _____

   _____

4. ***Twelfth Night*** (play):

   _____

   _____

   _____

5. ***The Adventures of Huckleberry Finn*** (book):

   _____

   _____

   _____

The Power of Language

Deborah Ellis uses language carefully to describe how Parvana feels when she is dressed as a girl in Afghanistan, and how she feels when dressed as a boy.

Directions: Review Chapter 1. Write down all of the negative words Ellis uses to show Parvana's feelings of fear and anxiety as she accompanies her father in the marketplace. The first one has been done for you.

slump		

Now, review Chapter 6. Write down all of the positive words Ellis uses to show Parvana's feelings of excitement and interest as she transforms into a boy. The first one has been done for you.

nice		

Finally, think of your favorite outfit and hairstyle. Below, write down nine words to describe them and the way they make you feel. Then, write a paragraph that describes you with this particular hairstyle and clothing.

Your Family Role

In Parvana's family, each person has a distinct role based, in part, on what jobs and chores they do.

Directions: Fill out their roles below. The first one has been done for you.

Name of Character	Role in Family
Father	He was a history professor and earned money reading and writing letters before his arrest.
Mother	
Nooria	
Parvana	
Maryam and Ali	

Now, think about your own family and the individual roles held by each member. Fill out the chart below with the names of your immediate family members, and brief descriptions of their roles. Don't forget to describe your own role!

Name of Family Member	Role in Family

Quiz Time

Answer the following questions about chapters 7–9.

1. What surprises Parvana about the Talib soldier with the letter?

_____

_____

2. Why does Parvana sell her beloved shalwar kameez?

_____

_____

3. Why does Mrs. Weera move in with Parvana's family?

_____

_____

4. Why do the children and women in Parvana's family finally get to go outside?

_____

_____

5. What does Parvana discover about one of the tea boys?

_____

_____

6. How does Parvana feel when Shauzia tells her that she probably won't hear from her father?

_____

_____

7. Why does Mrs. Weera want to start a school?

_____

_____

8. Why doesn't Parvana tell Shauzia about the embroidered handkerchief?

_____

_____

Embroidery

"One afternoon, when she was between customers, something landed on Parvana's head . . . .
a lovely white handkerchief with red embroidery around the edges."

Embroidery is an art involving decorative stitching on cloth. A handkerchief is a piece of cloth often used instead of disposable tissue. It's easy—and fun—to embroider a handkerchief of your own!

Materials

- one square of cotton or linen, 1' x 1'

- pinking shears

- paper and pencil

- embroidery thread in any color or colors

- an embroidery needle, one per student

Directions

1. Trim the edges of your cloth with pinking shears, all the way around, to prevent fraying of fabric. (Alternatively, you may press and sew a hem on all four sides.)

2. On your piece of paper, draw a design that you would like to embroider on your handkerchief.

3. Lightly draw this design onto your cloth with a pencil.

4. Thread your needle and begin embroidering. On the next page, you'll find pictures and descriptions of easy, popular stitches. When you are finished, display your handkerchief for all to enjoy!

Embroidery *(cont.)*

Running Stitch

This is the most simple embroidery stitch, used to create straight lines.

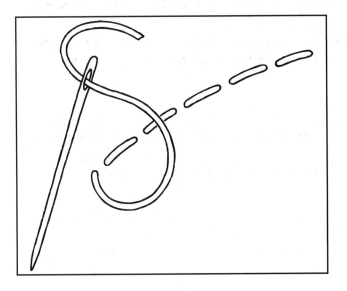

Satin Stitch

This is a series of flat stitches used to cover a background.

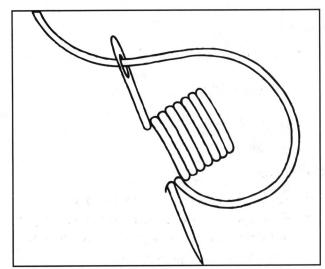

Cross-Stitch

This stitch is formed by making a series of Xs on a background.

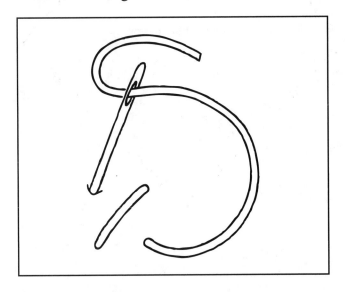

Chain Stitch

This is a stitch in which looped stitches form a chain.

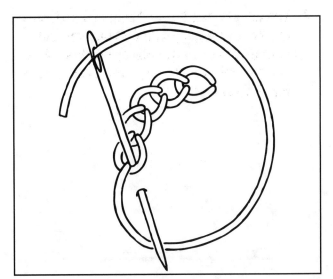

Create a Marketplace

The marketplace becomes an important location for Parvana. Here, she is able to make money from her skills as a reader and letter-writer. She can also buy nan bread and vegetables for her family.

To get a better understanding of the marketplace in Kabul, create a booth of your own and then go shopping at your classroom market!

Note to Teacher: decide before beginning this project whether students will hold their Class Marketplace outside or inside. Give students five pieces of representative money, such as dried beans or buttons, with which to "shop."

Directions

1. Break into groups of 3–4. First, decide what you will sell. Will it be a product that you make, such as origami birds or caricatures? Will you sell a skill, such as braiding hair or writing rhymed poetry? Or will you sell items that already exist, like candy or stickers? If you're selling objects, you'll need to create enough of them.

2. Discuss how much you will charge. Note that each shopper has five pieces of money. Parvana decides to tell people, "Pay whatever you like." Will you set a price at your booth, or will you allow people to pay whatever they like?

3. Design your booth. Parvana simply sets objects out on a blanket near a house. Other sellers have wooden stalls. What everyday objects can you use to make a booth? Where will you put your booth?

4. Decorate your booth and display what you are selling. How can you make your booth interesting to shoppers? What signs can you hang, and what objects can you set out so that people will stop and buy from you?

5. When all the booths are set up, it's time to shop. Decide which members of your group will work at your booth first, and which will go shopping. Make sure to trade roles so that everyone gets a chance to sell and to shop.

What's in Your Water?

> *"'This is the tap,' she said to her sister, as soon as they arrived. . . . 'Don't swallow any,' Parvana warned, then showed her how to splash her face with water."*

You may wonder why Parvana and her family aren't supposed to drink water unless they have boiled it first. In many parts of the world, water has been contaminated by oil, non-biodegradable detergents, trash, and other pollutants. Boiling water before drinking it kills germs.

Directions: To better understand how pollution affects water, answer the questions and do the activity on this page.

1. Why do you think the water in Parvana's city might be contaminated?

   _____

   _____

2. What do you think you might find in the water there that makes it unsafe to drink?

   _____

   _____

3. Do you think the water in your own city might be contaminated? Why/why not?

   _____

   _____

4. What do you think you might find in your city's water that makes it unsafe to drink?

   _____

   _____

Materials

- a clean 2-liter bottle with top
- water
- 1 cup of motor oil
- 1 cup non-biodegradable dish soap
- funnel

Directions

1. Pour three cups of water into the clean bottle. Explain that this represents a body of water, such as a lake, from which people get their water.
2. Pour oil into bottle via the funnel. Screw top on the bottle and shake.
3. Discuss what happens to the oil and water. Does the oil disappear or does it remain? Would you want to drink this water? How should oil be disposed?
4. Pour water and oil mixture into a can and recycle appropriately. Clean bottle.
5. Now, pour three cups of water into clean bottle. Pour one cup of non-biodegradable detergent into bottle via the funnel. Screw top on bottle and shake.
6. Discuss what happens to the detergent and water. Would you want to drink this water? How should non-biodegradable detergent be disposed?
7. Explain the concept of biodegradable detergent and soap. "Biodegradable" refers to products that break down quickly and disappear into the environment, such as a body of water, without harming it.

Writing a Letter

Parvana is surprised to feel sympathy for the Talib soldier who asks her to read his wife's letter. She sees the Taliban as the enemy, and yet she understands this man's individual sorrow over the loss of his wife.

Directions: Think about a time that someone said or did something you did not like. Below, write a letter from this person's point of view. Explain why this person said or did a particular thing, and how he/she felt about it afterward. Does seeing an action from his/her point of view change the way you feel about the person and the action?

Quiz Time

Answer the following questions about chapters 10–12.

1. How does Parvana feel about having to dig up bones?

_____

_____

2. Why is Parvana afraid to go to the bathroom at the cemetery?

_____

_____

3. Why does Parvana tell her family about digging up bones?

_____

_____

4. Why does Parvana continue to dig up bones, although it upsets her?

_____

_____

5. What do Parvana and Shauzia discover at the stadium?

_____

_____

6. Why does Parvana stay home after visiting the stadium?

_____

_____

7. Why does Shauzia want to go to France?

_____

_____

8. Why does Nooria's little school have to be a secret?

_____

_____

Plant a Flower Garden

Parvana and Shauzia are stuck in a city. Fields of flowers sound magical to them. You can plant a flower garden to add color and beauty to your surroundings.

Materials

- four planks, 4' x 8" x 1"
- four plastic or metal pointed-end brackets in which the edges of the planks fit to form a square

  (**Note:** Alternatively, you can build a flower bed from bricks, rocks, or other materials on hand.)
- at least three cubic feet of dirt—a mixture of soil, peat moss, and compost, if possible
- flower seeds
- 4-6 paper cups
- marker
- 4-6 wooden craft sticks

Directions

1. Decide where you will put your garden. Will it be in sun or shade? Is it near a water source? Build your plot from plants, bricks, rocks, or other materials.

2. Fill your plot at least ¾ full with soil.

3. Decide what flowers you will plant. Consider what types of flowers grow best in sun, partial shade, and full shade.

4. Label each paper cup with the type of flower you will plant. Place seeds in paper cups and fill half full with water. Soak the seeds overnight, to help them germinate in your soil.

5. Plot out your design. What flowers will go where? Will you include decorative statues and rocks? You may want to sketch your design on paper.

6. Plant your flower seeds, according to the directions on the packet. Note that you shouldn't plant them too deep in the soil, or they won't come up.

7. Write the name of each flower on a craft stick. Put the sticks in the soil to mark where you planted each type of flower.

8. Water your seeds. Keep the soil moist, but not soaking wet.

9. Seeds should sprout within a week to 10 days. Continue to water your flowers, and enjoy!

Make a Magazine

> *"In the end, Mother relented. 'You must tell me everything that happens,' she told Parvana. 'We will put it in the magazine, so that everyone will know.'"*

Mother and Mrs. Weera decide to start a magazine so that people around the world will know what is happening in Afghanistan.

You can make a magazine to let people know what is happening in your class.

Materials

- several sheets of 9" x 12" paper
- computer and printer, or pens and rulers
- photocopier (optional)
- three-hole puncher and three brads, or stapler

Directions

1. As a class, talk about what you want your magazine to look like. Do you want it to have departments such as Letters to the Editor, Fillers, Feature-Length Articles, Interviews, and Comics? Do you want it to have art and photographs? How many pages will your magazine contain? Choose a name for your magazine.

2. Break into groups of 3–4. Decide which department your group will work on, and how many pages you will create.

3. Decide what types of stories you'll include on your page, and what kinds of art you will include. What do you want people to know about your classroom and the students in it?

4. Write your stories and gather your art.

5. Now, put your pages together in one of two ways: you may choose to use a computer, and design your pages with a program such as Microsoft Word; or, you may want to handwrite your pages, creating columns with a ruler and markers.

6. If you decide to photocopy your magazine for distribution, do so at this point.

7. Finally, gather all finished magazine pages for one copy, or for several, into a stack. Bind each copy of your magazine with a three-hole punch and brads, or staple the pages together.

Land Mines

Parvana's older brother Hossain was killed by a land mine when he was fourteen years old. In the cemetery, she is afraid that an abandoned building might contain a land mine. *"Some were disguised as toys—special mines to blow up children."*

Land mines are responsible for thousands of deaths and injuries worldwide. Several groups are working hard to find and eliminate land mines.

Directions

Using books, encyclopedias, and the Internet, research the problem of land mines and answer the questions below.

1. What is a land mine?

   _____

   _____

2. Why do people set land mines in the ground?

   _____

   _____

3. How are people injured or killed by land mines?

   _____

   _____

4. What are the names of three countries that contain land mines?

   _____

   _____

5. Name one organization that is trying to ban land mines. What are people in this organization doing to help?

   _____

   _____

6. Research the late Princess Diana of Wales' work on the problem of land mines. How did she help to ban land mines?

   _____

   _____

7. What can you do to help rid the world of land mines?

   _____

   _____

Why We Do What We Do

In *The Breadwinner*, Parvana often does things she doesn't want to do, for the sake of her family. In your life, you likely do things that you don't want to, for the good of someone else.

Fill out the chart below, analyzing Parvana's actions and your own. The first one has been done for you.

Parvana's Actions	Why She Does Them
1. Fetches water	She fetches water because no one else in her family can. They need water to drink, and for cooking and cleaning.
2. Cuts off her hair	
3. Reads for Talib soldier	
4. Digs up bones	

Your Actions	Why You Do Them
1.	
2.	
3.	
4.	

Quiz Time

Answer the following questions about chapters 13–15.

1. Why is Nooria excited to move to Mazar-e-Sharif?

_____

_____

2. Why does Mother decide to leave Parvana in Kabul?

_____

_____

3. Why is the woman in the abandoned building afraid to go outside?

_____

_____

4. Why did Homa leave Mazar-e-Sharif?

_____

_____

5. Why is Parvana afraid for her family?

_____

_____

6. Why does Shauzia decide to leave Kabul?

_____

_____

7. Where are Mrs. Weera, Homa, and Shauzia going, and what will they do there?

_____

_____

8. Why does Parvana plant wildflowers in the marketplace?

_____

_____

Dried Apricots

"Parvana settled back in the truck beside her father. She popped a dried apricot into her mouth and rolled its sweetness around on her tongue."

Dried fruit is a treat in the poverty-ridden city of Kabul. Parvana sells bags of dried fruit and nuts in the marketplace. Below, you'll find a recipe for dried apricots that you can make and taste to find out why Parvana and her family enjoyed them so much!

Note: Check for food allergies before beginning this activity.

Ingredients

- 2–3 apricots per student
- water

Materials

- paring knife
- large bowl
- steamer basket
- large pot with lid
- two kitchen towels
- large, framed screen—a clean window screen works well
- spatula

Directions

1. Select your apricots. They must be ripe and free of blemishes. Wash them and cut them in half. Discard pits.

2. Blanch your apricots so they keep their color after they've dried. Fill large pot with two inches of water. Put burner on high. Place halved apricots in a steamer basket. When water is boiling, ask your teacher to place the basket in the pot for five minutes, with the lid on.

3. Drain the apricots and lay them on towels to dry.

4. Alternatively, you can dip your apricots in a blanching mixture instead of steaming them. Dip them in a mixture of 10 1-gram crushed vitamin C tablets mixed with one quart of water. Lay them on kitchen towels to dry.

5. Spread apricots on clean screen. Place them outside in the sun. Allow them to dry during the day, but bring them inside at night. Apricots will need to dry for 2–4 days, depending on the temperature outside. Midway through the drying process, flip apricots over on screen with spatula.

6. As an alternative, you can oven-dry your apricots. Preheat oven on its lowest temperature setting. Spread cheesecloth over oven racks and place fruit on it. Bake apricots between 4–12 hours until they are dry, but still chewable.

7. Store in an air-tight container. Enjoy!

   Note that this drying method works with cherries, apples, peaches, and other fruits as well!

A Helping Hand

Parvana and her family generously help Homa when she is discovered alone, frightened and poor. Think about a person, or a group of people, in your community who could benefit from your kind assistance. Are there children your age living in shelters who would enjoy crayons, paper, and small puzzles? What about a family who has lost their home in a fire? What could you offer to make their lives happier?

Directions

1. In groups of four, or as a class, choose a person or group of people to help. Look in your local phone book or on the Internet to find appropriate contact information. Note that if you've chosen to help an organization, you should begin by contacting the director. You can often locate contact information for families in need by looking for their story in the local newspaper.

2. Discuss what this person or group of people needs most. If clothes are needed, consider donating an item you no longer wear. Do the same with toys and books. If you decide that this person or group most needs food, you can host a canned-food drive at your school and make gift baskets of food in cans and well-sealed original packaging. Perhaps you'll find that what this person or group needs is your time. Decide how many hours you'll spend on this project, and make arrangements for specific days and times to offer your assistance.

3. Finally, meet back in your group to discuss the results of your project. Answer the questions below.

---

1. What did your group offer this person or group of people?

   _____

   _____

   _____

2. What was this person's or group's reaction to your generosity?

   _____

   _____

   _____

3. How did you feel as you offered care to this person or group of people?

   _____

   _____

   _____

What They Wear

Men and women in Kabul dress very differently from one another. Parvana completely changes her appearance so that people will believe she is a boy.

Directions: Using books, encyclopedias, and/or the Internet, research the different types of clothing worn by males and females in Kabul, Afghanistan. Then, draw an Afghan man and woman in the spaces below. Label items of clothing with the appropriate word such as "burqa" or "chador."

Afghan Man	Afghan Women

You and Parvana

By the end of *The Breadwinner*, you may find that your life is very different from that of Parvana's.

Directions: Fill out the statements below to better understand the differences and similarities between your life and Parvana's life.

1. While Parvana is proud that she can help her family, I am proud that

_____

_____

2. Parvana is allowed to work at 11 years old, while I am allowed to

_____

_____

3. A treat for Parvana is the sweet taste of dried apricots. For me, a treat is

_____

_____

4. At Parvana's age, many girls get married and start families. At my age, kids

_____

_____

5. Parvana and her family live together in one room, while my family

_____

_____

6. Parvana plants wildflowers in the marketplace to create something beautiful, while I

_____

_____

Any Questions?

When you finished reading *The Breadwinner*, you surely had questions that were left unanswered. Write a few of your questions on the back of this paper.

Work in groups or alone to predict possible answers for some or all of the questions you asked on the back of this page, as well as for those written below. When you have finished, share your predictions with your class.

1. What happens to Mother, Nooria, and the rest of the family? _____
   _____

2. Does Shauzia get to France? _____

3. What experiences do Parvana and Father have as they travel north? _____
   _____

4. What happens to Mrs. Weera and Homa? _____
   _____

5. What does Shauzia's family do when they discover she is gone? _____
   _____

6. Does Parvana have to get married at a young age?_____

7. Do soldiers eventually discover that Parvana is a girl?_____

8. Does Parvana stay dressed like a boy because she has more freedom this way?_____

9. What happens to the room Parvana shared with her family? _____
   _____

10. What happens to the Window Woman who gave Parvana gifts? _____
    _____

11. How does Mother's and Mrs. Weera's magazine affect change in the world?_____
    _____

12. Does Parvana go back to school? _____

13. What happens to Afghanistan? Do its people finally live in peace? _____
    _____

14. How does Parvana change as she travels north with her sick father?_____
    _____

15. Do Parvana and her father find the rest of their family?_____

16. Is Nooria happy in Mazar-e-Sharif? _____

17. Do Nooria and Parvana eventually become close? _____

18. What does Parvana become when she grows up? _____

19. What happens to Maryam? Does she also begin to dress like a boy? _____
    _____

20. What stories do the Afghans tell about Parvana in the future? _____
    _____

21. Do the Taliban soldiers ever realize the number of girls dressed like boys in Afghanistan?
    _____

Book Report Ideas

There are several ways to report on a book after you have read it. When you have finished *The Breadwinner,* choose a method of reporting from the list below, or come up with your own idea on how best to report on this book.

Make a Book Jacket

Design a book jacket for this book. On the front, draw a picture that you feel best captures this story. On the back, write a paragraph or two which summarizes the main points of this book.

Make a Time Line

On paper, create a time line to show the significant events in Parvana's life. Illustrate your time line.

Design a Scrapbook

Use magazine pictures, photographs, and other illustrations to create a scrapbook that Parvana or another character might keep to document her life. She might choose to decorate her scrapbook with pressed wildflowers, her old chador, a bag she has used for nuts and dried fruit, and some of the gifts given to her by the Window Woman.

Make a Collage

Using old magazines and photographs, design a collage that illustrates the challenges faced by Parvana's family in Afghanistan.

Create a Time Capsule

What items might one character from *The Breadwinner* put in a time capsule by which to document Kabul under Taliban rule? What particular container might this character use as a time capsule?

Write a Biography

Do research to find out about the life of author Deborah Ellis. You may use the Internet or magazines. Write a biography, showing how Deborah's own experiences might have influenced her writing of *The Breadwinner.*

Act Out a Play

With one or two other students, write a play featuring some of the characters in this novel. Then act out your play for your class.

Make Puppets

Using a variety of materials, design puppets to represent one or all of the characters in *The Breadwinner.* You may decide to work with other students to write and perform a puppet show.

Research Ideas

As you read *The Breadwinner*, you discovered geographical locations, events, and people about which you might wish to know more! To increase your understanding of the characters, places, and events in this novel, do research to discover additional information.

Work alone or in groups to discover more about one or several of the items listed below. You may use books, magazines, encyclopedias, and the Internet to do your research. When you are finished, share your discoveries with your class.

- Afghanistan
- Kabul
- Mazar-e-Sharif
- the Taliban
- women's rights organizations in Afghanistan
- Afghan wars
- land mines
- human rights
- treatment of women in Afghanistan
- loss of jobs in Afghanistan
- traditional Kabul marketplaces
- foods of Afghanistan
- living conditions in Afghanistan
- marriage age of young people in Afghanistan
- Kabul before and after Taliban rule
- wildflowers of Afghanistan

- magazines devoted to human-rights issues
- curfews
- France
- graveyard robberies
- Afghan schools
- traditional Afghan embroidery
- the story of Malali
- bride-prices
- geography of Afghanistan
- United States aid to Afghanistan
- Afghan refugees
- literacy in Afghanistan
- water pollution
- traditional gender roles in Afghanistan
- weather in Afghanistan
- the importance of tea in Afghanistan

A Celebration of Afghanistan

Afghanistan is much more than bombed out buildings, soldiers, and impoverished people. You can plan and host a celebration of Afghanistan to show the richness and beauty of this culture.

Party Checklist

Three weeks before the party . . .

❑ Decide when and where the party will occur.

❑ Discuss how to create an Afghan-themed party. Parvana and her family eat on the floor. They eat particular foods and wear particular clothing. How would Parvana, her parents, and her siblings dress when they celebrate in their house? Can you wear something similar and play Afghan music and games?

❑ Do you want to invite guests to your party? If so, make and send invitations.

❑ Discuss decorations. Parvana has a fondness for wildflowers. What other articles can you use as decorations with an Afghan theme? Perhaps you'll want to put up your Afghanistan time lines from page 13, your puzzles from page 17, or your embroidered handkerchiefs from page 22.

Two weeks before the party . . .

❑ Decide what food and drink you will make as a class. This book provides recipes for nan bread, dried apricots, and khatai cookies. Tea would also be appropriate.

❑ Pass around a sign-up sheet. Each student should bring something unique to the celebration. Consider bringing different foods from Afghanistan, play an Afghan song on an instrument, bring an object for show-and-tell, or lead an Afghan game from page 42.

❑ Send home a note to students' parents to let them know the day/date of the party, as well as what the student signed up to bring or do.

One week before the party . . .

❑ Make decorations and dried apricots.

❑ Make and freeze khatai cookies.

The day of the party . . .

❑ Decorate the party space.

❑ Make nan bread.

❑ Put on Afghan music.

    Enjoy!

Khatai Cookies

These delicious cookies are popular in Afghanistan, as well as in Pakistan and India.

Makes approximately 40 cookies.

Note: Please check for food allergies before using this recipe.

Ingredients

- 3 cups white flour
- 2 cups sugar
- 1½ cups corn oil
- 1 T crushed cardamom powder
- butter for greasing cookie sheets
- 1 cup hulled pistachios

Materials

- oven
- large bowl
- mixing spoon or electric mixer
- small spoon
- cookie sheets
- spatula
- cookie racks
- food processor or blender

Directions

1. Preheat over to 350 degrees. Grease cookie sheets.
2. Mix flour with sugar and cardamom powder. Add corn oil and mix well.
3. Form dough into 2" balls. Place them on cookie sheets, 1" apart.
4. Bake for 15 minutes, or until lightly browned.
5. While cookies are baking, finely grind pistachios in food processor or blender.
6. When cookies are finished, sprinkle them with pistachios.
7. Place cookies on racks to cool. Enjoy with tea.

How to Steep Tea

Even at age 11, Parvana surely knows the tricks to steeping a good cup of loose-leaf tea.

Directions:

1. Use only spring or filtered water.
2. Do not let the water come to a full boil.
3. Pour the water over the tea leaves in a pot and cover.
4. Infuse your tea for three to five minutes. Serve in tea cups.

Two Afghan Games

You might want to play these at your Celebration of Afghanistan.

Top Danda

This is a game played between two teams. It is similar to baseball.

Materials

- a tennis ball
- sidewalk chalk

Directions:

1. Separate the class into two teams. Decide which will play defense first, and which will play offense.

2. Draw two large circles about 100 feet from one another. The defending team stands inside the circle while the offending team stands outside.

3. Assign each person inside the circle a number. Number one "bats" first, number two "bats" second, and so on. Assign a pitcher on the other team.

4. Now, the pitcher throws the tennis ball to the number one "batter" in the circle. This player gets one chance to hit it out of the circle with an open hand. If the player hits the ball, he/she must run to the other circle.

5. Now, the number two "batter" tries to hit the ball. If successful, he/she runs to other circle while the first "batter" tries to return to the original circle.

6. During the batting, defensive players outside the circle attempt to catch the ball. If the ball is caught, the "batter" is out of the game.

7. They may also toss the ball gently at a runner below the knees. If the runner is tapped by the ball outside the circle, he/she must also leave the game.

8. When all of the offensive "batters" are out, the other team lines up inside the circle to "bat."

Jiz-Bazee (American variation)

This is a popular game in Afghanistan, similar to hopscotch.

Materials

- sidewalk chalk
- a small, smooth stone called a lishp in Afghanistan.

Directions:

1. On the sidewalk or blacktop, draw eight connected squares in a circle. Number them 1–8.

2. Standing three feet from the squares, the first person throws the lishp into square 1. If this player is successful, he/she throws the lishp into square 2, and so on until all the squares have been touched. If not, the next player gets to try.

   A variation: Children in Afghanistan also take turns trying to close their eyes and step carefully through all the squares, from 1 to 8, without stepping on a line. If the player steps on a line, the next player gets to try.

Objective Test and Essay

Matching: Match the descriptions of the characters with their names.

_____ **1.** Parvana

_____ **2.** Mother

_____ **3.** Nooria

_____ **4.** Maryem

_____ **5.** Hossain

_____ **6.** Mrs. Weera

_____ **7.** Shauzia

_____ **8.** Father

_____ **9.** Homa

a. wants to move to France and not get married

b. killed by a land mine at age 14

c. agrees to marriage, in part for the freedom to go to school

d. plants wildflowers in the marketplace

e. moves to Pakistan with Homa

f. loses part of a leg and goes to prison

g. is a writer who helps to start a magazine

h. is a little girl who hasn't been outside in a year-and-a-half

i. flees Mazar-e-Sharif after her family is killed

True or False: Answer true or false in the blanks below.

_____ **1.** It is not dangerous for Parvana's family to travel from Kabul to Mazar-e-Sharif.

_____ **2.** Nooria doesn't want to get married to the boy she knew in school.

_____ **3.** Parvana and Nooria gradually develop a more positive relationship in the novel.

_____ **4.** Mother is eager to go out into the streets of Kabul.

_____ **5.** Parvana becomes the breadwinner for her family.

Short Answer: Write a brief response, 2–3 sentences, on separate paper.

1. How is Parvana treated differently on the streets depending on whether she is dressed as male or female?

2. Why does Mother fall into a deep depression for days?

3. What does Mrs. Weera do to help women in Afghanistan?

4. How have Taliban laws changed Kabul?

Essay: Respond to the following on separate paper.

At the beginning of this book, Parvana is one type of person. She changes into a different type of person by the end of the book. In a short essay, explain how Parvana changes and why.

Responding to Quotes

On a separate page, explain the context of the following quotes as selected by yourself or by your teacher.

Chapter One: "As a small girl, she could usually get away with being outside without being questioned."

Chapter Two: "'The lesson here, my daughters,' he looked from one to the other, 'is that Afghanistan has always been home to the bravest women in the world.'"

Chapter Three: "'I will not walk around my own city with a note pinned to my burqa as if I were a kindergarten child. I have a university degree!'"

Chapter Four: "'We're out of food.' There was no response. 'Mother, there's no food left.'"

Chapter Five: "'Fetch the bucket, girl. Do your bit for the team. Here we go!' Mrs. Weera still talked like she was out on the hockey field, urging everyone to do their best."

Chapter Six: "They were going to turn her into a boy."

Chapter Seven: "Parvana was about to squish her eyes shut and wait to be shot when she saw that the Talib had taken out a letter."

Chapter Eight: "Maryam had seen nothing but the four walls of their room for almost a year-and- a-half."

Chapter Nine: "A couple of tea boys heard of a way to make money. Lots of money."

Chapter Ten: "Taking a deep breath and uttering a quick prayer, she stepped through the doorway. She did not explode."

Chapter Eleven: "'These men are thieves,' the soldiers called out to the crowd. 'See how we punish thieves? We cut off one of their hands!'"

Chapter Twelve: "France. I'll get on a boat and go to France."

Chapter Thirteen: "At least in Mazar I can go to school, walk the streets without having to wear a burqa, and get a job when I've completed school."

Chapter Fourteen: "'Where is your burqa?' She looked around but couldn't see one. 'Are you outside without a burqa?'"

Chapter Fifteen: "'The boy has undertaken to bring a bit of beauty into our gray marketplace, and do you thank him? Do you help him?'"

Conversations

Work in groups according to the numbers in parenthesis. Act out the conversations that might have occurred in each of the following situations in *The Breadwinner*.

- Parvana meets up with Nooria near Mazar-e-Sharif. (2 people)

- Father and Mother reunite in Mazar. (2 people)

- Parvana tells her father all that has happened since he went to prison. (2 people)

- Shauzia and Parvana meet at the top of the Eiffel Tower. (2 people)

- Maryam grows up and tells Ali about how Parvana saved the family. (2 people)

- Nooria and her new husband talk about why Parvana's hair is so short. (2 people)

- Mother tells Parvana how she feels about her son who was killed by a land mine. (2 people)

- Mrs. Weera and Homa talk about their plans to organize Afghan women refugees on the way to Pakistan. (2 people)

- The sad Taliban soldier tells his friends about the boy who read the letter from his dead wife. (3 people)

- Parvana, Maryam, and Ali talk about getting to go to school again. (3 people)

- Mother, Nooria, and Father talk about whether they should move out of Afghanistan. (3 people)

- Mrs. Weera tells Parvana and Nooria how to best take care of her mother during her depression. (3 people)

- Parvana and Shauzia tell Maryam why it's important to learn to read and write. (3 people)

- Mrs. Weera and Mother tell Nooria, Parvana, and Maryam what Afghanistan used to be like for women who lived there. (4 people)

- Father and Ali meet two Taliban soldiers in the marketplace. (4 people)

Bibliography of Related Reading

Fiction

Ellis, Deborah. *A Company of Fools.* Groundwood, 2004. Ellis, Deborah. *The Heaven Shop.* Groundwood, 2004.

– – –*Mud City.* Groundwood, 2004.

– – –*Parvana's Journey.* Groundwood, 2003.

Munoz, Pam. *Esperanza Rising.* Blue Sky, 2002.

Nye, Naomi Shihab. *Habibi.* Simon Pulse, 1999.

Staples, Suzanne Fisher. *Haveli.* Laurel Leaf, 1995.

– – –*Under the Persimmon Tree.* Farrar, Straus & Giroux, 2005.

Stolz, Joelle. *The Shadow of Ghadames.* Yearling, 2006.

Whelan, Gloria. *Homeless Bird.* HarperTrophy, 2001.

Non-Fiction

Banting, Erinn. *Afghanistan: The Culture.* Crabtree, 2003.

– – –*Afghanistan: The Land.* Crabtree, 2003.

– – –*Afghanistan: The People.* Crabtree, 2003.

Barth, Kelly. *At Issue in History: The Rise and Fall of the Taliban.* Greenhaven, 2004.

Behnke, Alison. *Afghanistan in Pictures.* Lerner, 2003.

Ellis, Deborah. *Three Wishes: Palestinian and Israeli Children Speak.* Groundwood, 2006.

Olson, Gillia M. and Abdul Raheem Yaseer. *Afghanistan.* Fact Finders, 2004.

Rifa'i, Amal and Odelia Ainbinder. *We Just Want to Live Here: A Palestinian Teenager, an Israeli Teenager—An Unlikely Friendship.* St. Martin's Griffin, 2003.

Steward, Gail. *The Way People Live—Life Under the Taliban.* Lucent, 2004.

Web Sites

http://www.educationworld.com (type in the search term Afghanistan)

http://en.wikipedia.org/wiki/Category:Educational_websites (type in the search terms Afghanistan, Kabul, Taliban)

Answer Key

Page 11

1. Parvana isn't supposed to be outside because Taliban soldiers have ordered women and girls to stay inside.
2. Parvana's father sells the family's objects, and reads and writes letters for money.
3. Parvana's family lives together in one small room because their homes have been bombed, and they have become progressively poorer.
4. Parvana is the only person in her family who can fetch water because her sisters and Mother can't be out on the street, her brother is too young, and her Father is injured.
5. Afghans are supposed to treat a guest with generosity, offering the best that they have.
6. Malali is a young girl who led Afghan troops in the fight against British soldiers in 1880.
7. The Taliban take Father away because he went to England for his education and they don't like his foreign ideas.
8. Parvana is afraid that if she loses track of her mother on the street, she'll never find her again because all women look the same in their burqas and chadors.

Page 13

Note that answers will differ in terms of what events strike students as most important. Some significant events in Afghan history include: (1709) Mirwais Khan Hotak kills Persian-appointed governor Gurgin Khan and declares himself King of Afghanistan; (1809) Afghan king Shuja Shah Durrani signs a treaty of alliance with the United Kingdom; (1839) First Anglo-Afghan War; (1921) Afghanistan defeats Britain and becomes an independent nation; (1965) Marxist People's Democratic Party of Afghanistan holds its first congress; (1979) Soviet army invades Afghanistan; (1989) Last Soviet troops leave Afghanistan; (1995) Islamic militia called the Taliban rises to power; (2001) Members of al-Qaeda, headquartered in Afghanistan, commit terrorist attacks on the U.S., whose soldiers then begin to bomb the country; (2002) NATO expands its peacekeeping operation into southern Afghanistan.

Page 14

1. Afghanistan is located in Asia. Its closest neighbors are Pakistan, Iran, Turkmenistan, Uzbekistan, and Tajikistan.
2. In Afghanistan, people speak Farsi, Dari, Pashto, and dozens of other languages.
3. People in Afghanistan play Buzkashi, tent-pegging, kite-fighting, topay-danda, wrestling, boxing, martial arts, basketball, soccer, archery, and bicycle racing.
4. Poetry is recited at most social events in Afghanistan. The ability to write and narrate it is very much admired. Poetry has a long history in this country. The great poet Rumi came from Afghanistan, beginning a centuries-long tradition of this form of writing.
5. These days, both boys and girls can go to school in Afghanistan. However, schools face a lack of teachers and textbooks, as well as buildings. Security issues are also a problem. In 2007, about half of Afghanistan's children attended school.
6. In Afghanistan, people eat nan bread, chutney, spinach, rice, salad, kabobs, yogurt sauce, ice cream, cheese with raisins, nuts, dried fruit, tea, etc.
7. In Afghanistan, you would find leopards, tigers, black bears, otters, bats, goats, porcupines, mongooses, flying squirrels, shrews, and many others.
8. Afghanistan is landlocked and mountainous, with four major rivers, and several smaller rivers and lakes.

Page 15

Parvana shows resentment because she has to fetch water for the family. She shows anger because the Taliban have changed her way of life. She is fearful when her father gets taken to prison, and her mother grows depressed. She is also afraid when she has to go to the marketplace as a girl. She shows happiness when she can earn money and shop for her family, and when the Window-Woman gives her gifts. She is also happy to see her father when he returns.

Page 16

1. Father wants Mother to go out into the city so that she can write about what she sees.
2. Mother sleeps for so long and stays silent because she is depressed at the imprisonment of her husband, at the death of her son, and at the problems in her country.
3. Parvana finally goes out in search of food because the family is hungry and she is the only person who can safely go outside.
4. The Talib solider hits Parvana with a stick because she is a girl outside in the marketplace.
5. Mother and Mrs. Weera met in the Afghan Women's Union.
6. The family, along with Mrs. Weera, decides to turn Parvana into a boy because then she can make money and shop for the family.
7. Parvana discovers that she has more freedom. She isn't singled out, and the Taliban soldiers leave her alone.
8. Parvana has to look like a boy inside, when she is with her family, so that Taliban soldiers will think that there is a young male adult living in the house with the women.

Page 18

2. Mulan dresses like a boy and goes to war for her father because he is too old to fight and has no sons.
3. Michael Dorsey can't find work as an actor, so he dresses like a woman to audition for a female part in a soap opera. He gets the role.
4. Viola dresses as a boy after she is shipwrecked and loses her twin brother. As a man, she works as a page for a duke.
5. Huckleberry Finn disguises himself as a girl so that he can run away from the Widow Douglas and get information about Jim, an escaped slave.

Page 19

Ellis uses the following words to describe Parvana when she is dressed like a girl in the marketplace: *whispered, hiding, afraid, invisible, uncomfortable, missed, angry, slowly.* She uses the following words to describe Parvana when she is dressed like a boy: *soft, nice, beautiful, confident, open, boldly, proud, burst, good, ran.*

Page 20

Mother cooks and cleans and takes care of the children.

Nooria helps Mother to cook and clean and care for the children.

Parvana helps Father to walk to and from the marketplace. Later, she earns money, shops, and escorts her family outside.

Maryam and Ali are too young to have many tasks yet. They are the children in the family. Maryam tries to help around the house.

Page 21

1. Parvana is surprised because the Talib soldier is sad, and she feels sympathy for him.
2. Parvana sells her beloved shalwar kameez to a man so that she has money to feed her family.
3. Mrs. Weera moves in with Parvana's family partially to help, and partially because her own room is small and she is living with just her toddler son.

Answer Key (cont.)

4. The children and women in Parvana's family finally get to go outside because Parvana, dressed as a boy, accompanies them.

5. *Parvana* discovers that one of the tea boys is her female friend, Shauzia.

6. Parvana feels angry and scared when Shauzia tells her that she probably won't hear from her father.

7. Mrs. Weera wants to start a school to educate Afghan women and girls who aren't allowed to go to public school.

8. This is open to interpretation. Parvana might not tell Shauzia about the embroidered handkerchief because she wants to keep the gifts or the secret of the Window Woman to herself.

Page 25

1. The water in Parvana's city might be contaminated due to poor sanitation, bombings, and polluted waterways due to lack of waste management services.

2. In Afghanistan, you might find harmful bacteria in the water, as well as oil, detergent, and other undrinkable substances.

3. This is open to student interpretation and understanding.

4. Students might identify pollution and bacteria in their city's water supply, depending on their level of awareness and research.

Page 26

Accept all reasonable letters that demonstrate effort.

Page 27

1. Parvana hates having to dig up bones. She feels sad and scared.

2. Parvana is afraid to go to the bathroom at the cemetery because the building might hold land mines.

3. Parvana tells her family about digging up bones because the experience has made her so uncomfortable.

4. Parvana continues to dig up bones, although it upsets her, because the money is good and she wants to buy a tray from which to sell candy and cigarettes.

5. Parvana and Shauzia discover Taliban soldiers cutting the hands off supposed Afghan thieves at the stadium.

6. Parvana stays home after visiting the stadium because she is scared and depressed over the actions of the soldiers.

7. Shauzia wants to go to France because she hears that it is a beautiful, friendly country where she can walk into a field of flowers and not have to think.

8. Nooria's little school has to be a secret because the Taliban forbid girls to go to school.

Page 30

1. A land mine is an explosive device set just under the ground.

2. People set land mines in the ground to injure and kill soldiers and civilians from opposing countries/territories.

3. When land mines explode, they rip apart bodies which causes death or injury.

4. Some countries that contain land mines are Afghanistan, Cambodia, Angola, and Bosnia.

5. There are several organizations involved in trying to ban land mines. A few are stoplandmines.org, International Campaign to Ban Land Mines, and the Swiss Foundation for Mine Action. Members send money to help victims, work closely with governments, and do public outreach/education.

6. Princess Diana of Wales visited several countries devastated by land mines. She met victims, raised public awareness of the problem, and campaigned to ban land mines.

7. Students should realize that they can send letters to local politicians, as well as letters of support to various organizations. They may also want to do outreach and education at their school, and conduct a fundraiser to send money to one of the organizations they've researched.

Page 31

2. She cuts off her hair because she realizes that as a boy, she will be able to provide her family with money and food.

3. She reads the letter for the Talib soldier because she needs to make money, and she doesn't want to arouse suspicion. She also feels sympathy for him.

4. She digs up bones in order to earn more money to buy a tray from which to sell candy and cigarettes.

Page 32

1. Nooria is excited to move to Mazar-e-Sharif because she can go to school and walk outside freely.

2. Mother decides to leave Parvana in Kabul because she won't be able to explain why her daughter looks like a boy.

3. The woman in the abandoned building is safraid to go outside because she doesn't have a burqa or a chador.

4. Homa left Mazar-e-Sharif because Taliban soldiers killed her family. She was afraid for her life.

5. Parvana is afraid that Taliban soldiers will kill her family on their trip up north.

6. Shauzia decides to leave Kabul because her family wants her to get married.

7. Mrs. Weera, Homa, and Shauzia are going to Pakistan to work with a woman's group organizing Afghan women in exile.

8. Parvana plants wildflowers in the marketplace to give the Window Woman hope and beauty while she is away.

Page 43

Matching

1. d	4. h	7. a
2. g	5. b	8. f
3. c	6. e	9. i

True or False

1. False	4. False
2. False	5. True
3. True	

Short Answer

1. Parvana is beaten and yelled at as a female, while as a male she is ignored and has the freedom to shop and sell objects and services.

2. Mother falls into a deep depression for days because her son has been killed, her husband has been thrown into prison, she has lost her job, and her family is destitute.

3. Mrs. Weera helps to start a magazine and a school, and she moves to Pakistan to help women organize for human rights.

4. Taliban laws have kept women inside, forbidden them to go to school and shop, and have caused people to lose their jobs. They have imposed strict curfews, and they cultivate a mindset of fear.

Essay: Parvana is initially resentful of her sister and angry that she always has to fetch water. She feels helpless and scared. In the course of the novel, she gains confidence and courage. She grows compassionate and acts with kindness and bravery.

Page 44

Grade students on comprehension of the story as evidenced by the length of answers and depth of responses.

Page 45

Grade students on comprehension of the story, knowledge of the characters, and creativity.